Maiden

to

Mother

Letters for the Journey

by

Mel Spittall

Her WildLife Press

For permission requests, contact:

Her WildLife Press

Gold Coast, Queensland, Australia

www.herwildlife.com.au

First Edition, 2025

ISBN: 978-0-646-73001-1

Edited and designed in alignment with Natural Lore and Her
WildLife Press.

Printed in Australia by Lulu Press.

⊚

For my daughter Asha, on her 18th trip around the sun.

Your name carries the remembrance of truth, the renewal of hope, and the continuation of life through lineage.

You arrived when I was still remembering who I was, and in every way, you called me home.

May these words remind you that life will keep asking you to rise, to soften, to trust.

And that even when I am not beside you, my love moves through you, as breath, as blood, and as the quiet knowing that you were always meant to walk your own way.

⊚

PREFACE

There's a whisper I've felt my whole life.
Sometimes it came as a soft knowing at sunrise, walking home barefoot after a night of music and too much red wine. Sometimes it arrived as aching bones and an unnamed grief, through the wild eyes of a horse or the hush of wind moving through trees. A voice I didn't recognise, but never questioned.

I know now it was you.

These letters are for you, my daughter. But they're also for the girl I used to be, for the women I meet in the field, for the mothers who don't yet have words for what they've carried, and for the maidens still learning to protect their own magic.

This isn't a memoir. It's a transmission.

Drawn from journals I've kept since I was a girl, this book is stitched from my own rites of passage, the ones no one named for me. The heartbreaks I romanticised. The friendships that saved me. The descent into shadow. The quiet return to something ancient and whole. The land that held me. The horses that saw me. The truth I tried to forget and the one I couldn't stop remembering.

In writing these letters, I'm not just telling you my story, I'm telling you yours, before you even live it.

Not so you'll follow my footsteps, but so you'll recognise the terrain if you get there.

These letters follow the rhythm of my own becoming and my own remembering, not as a timeline to follow, but as a mirror to recognise yourself in, no matter your age. They are not just words, but maps made of stardust, dirt, and memory. They're here to remind you, and every woman who finds this book, that the passage from maiden to mother is not about age, but about awakening, claiming, and choosing to remember what was never actually lost.

So if you find yourself aching, searching, spiralling, or burning, come sit with me.

I've kept a fire going.

Sometimes I feel them moving through me
the mothers of my mother's line,
the ones who swallowed their truth
so their daughters could one day speak it.
They move beneath my skin
like roots remembering the way home to water.
When I breathe, the land exhales.
I am their remembering.
The wind whispers: begin.

CHAPTER ONE

The Girl Who Burned Too Bright

Letters for the edge of longing, magic, and undoing

Letter One: The Reckless One

To the daughter I might one day meet

Dear daughter,

When you read this, know it was written from a time when I barely knew who I was.

I had just left home. The ache in my chest felt like freedom and also like something I wasn't quite ready for. I chased music and moonlight, barefoot in backstreets, dancing in kitchens with friends who felt like lifelines and strangers who felt like spells.

We drank too much and slept too little. We smoked cigarettes and lay in fields talking about the universe. There was always someone I loved who didn't love me back, and someone who loved me that I couldn't even see.

I was surrounded by people, yet lonelier than I'd ever been. And still, those nights were magic, the kind that hurts a little. Everything shimmered. Everything ached. I thought that was normal. I thought love was supposed to ache. That longing meant it was real. I hadn't yet learned that being *wanted* isn't the same as being *held*.

There was one boy.

He wasn't mine, not really.

But I let him crawl into all the empty spaces and name them love.

Maybe it was the way he fixed his gaze on me as he crossed the dance floor, like I should already know who he was. Maybe it was that I looked away first and how no one ever made me do that. Maybe it was his stage presence, the room on fire, his voice like smoke under my skin. The way he spoke, low and close, like a secret. Like I was the only one who got to see the softness beneath the swagger.

He was taller than me. Older. Witty. Charismatic. A smart-arse, really. But he made me laugh, and I was starved for that kind of laughter, the kind that makes you forget you're trying so hard to be lovable.

He was intoxicating. Mystery and heat and detachment all at once. When he touched my arm, the fire in my belly would rise to my chest and I'd feel faint and floaty and a little sick.

So of course I thought it meant love.

The not-knowing hooked me. The maybe, the mixed signals, the almosts. I bent myself into shapes I thought he'd find more beautiful. Almost-love. Almost-worthiness. Almost being seen.

I didn't realise yet that when someone is really into you, there's no confusion. No waiting. No decoding looks and silences.

But I was eighteen, and I romanticised everything. It's a curse I think, the way I turned even my own heartbreak into poetry; the way I called it fate when it was really just loneliness dressed in eyeliner.

I learned from that ache how quickly I could give myself away; how easily I confused intensity with intimacy; how desperate I was to be loved, so much so that I couldn't see the ones who actually did. Most importantly, I learned that the most sacred parts of myself, the parts I handed out like gifts, were the very parts I needed to keep close.

It took years for me to stop chasing people who didn't want to stay. To stop proving my worth by how much I could endure. To stop bleeding out my softness for those not ready to receive it.

And maybe that's why I'm writing this now. Not to warn you away from love, but to tell you that you are already enough without it.

You want connection? Ache if you must.
But don't shrink yourself to fit inside someone else's maybe.
Let them rise to meet you.

I didn't know you then. But in the hush between songs, or the long walk home at dawn, I'd feel a thread tugging. Warm, wise, waiting.

Maybe it was you.

Maybe you've always been there, watching me from a distance, not to judge me, but to understand where your own story might begin.

This is where the journey of these letters begins. Not with certainty. Not with clarity. But with the sweet ache of a girl who was trying so hard to find home in someone else's eyes.

Let this be a map, not a rule. Take what you need. Burn the rest.

With all the love I didn't yet know how to hold,
Your mother *xx*

Letter Two: The Ache in the Dark

To the daughter who will walk through her own shadows

Dear daughter,

Not all of my late teens was music and midnight. Some nights cracked open without warning. I'd lie on the floor in a stranger's house and feel the whole world move without me.

Loneliness hurts differently when you don't know who you are yet. It makes some things feel hollow, even laughter, even kisses, even when someone says your name and you still don't feel seen.

Some nights I wrote about death, not because I didn't want to be alive, but because I didn't know how to live. Not fully. Not honestly. Not in a way that didn't involve shape-shifting to survive.

I thought the ache was just part of being human. Maybe it is. But I also think we inherit silence. We carry the grief of women who didn't get to scream, and when there's nowhere for it to go, it stays.

"The end of living, the beginning of survival."

That line haunted me for years. It felt like a performance of a life: moments I was supposed to enjoy but mostly endured.

And yet, even then, I still believed in magic.

There were whispers in the trees at night. There was power in the wind slipping through my curtains, cooling my skin, reminding me I was still here, still breathing, even when everything inside felt unclear and undone.

I wondered why I couldn't just be happy; why I felt so deeply; why sadness lingered when nothing seemed wrong. I didn't know it then, but my body was trying to protect me. It thought happiness was a trick. That calm was just the pause before the chaos. That safety was something I hadn't earned yet.

Some days I wore the ache like a second skin. Other days I wrapped it in poetry:

> *"A soft sea mist drifts through amber street lights.*
> *Salty tears descend down burning skin.*
> *Do I deserve this?"*

I'd write lines like that with a cigarette between my fingers, half-crying, half-mystic, wanting to be loved but not wanting to be seen.

I didn't have an answer. Only this: I was trying to feel alive.

If you find yourself in the dark, where your body is heavy and your heart feels like a stranger's, know this: you are not broken. You're feeling what others won't let themselves feel. You are a deep well. A thunderstorm. A priestess in training. You are the storm and the shelter.

Let your ache speak, but don't let it name you.

Somewhere inside that darkness, I gathered light. Laughter with friends, a dog brushing my arm, eucalyptus in the rain. They didn't fix me; they reminded me I didn't need fixing.

The pain isn't punishment and your depth isn't a flaw. It's your gift. Your compass. Proof you're still here.

With all the softness I once thought was weakness, Your mother *xx*

Letter Three: The Witch Who Remembered

To the daughter who senses the unseen

Dear daughter,

I used to whisper it like a secret spell: *"I think I'm a witch."*

Not the Halloween kind. The kind who hears what others don't. Who feels truth in her body before the mind catches up. Who cries under full moons for reasons she can't name.

I don't know when I first knew.
Maybe it was when I stood in the rain as a child, arms stretched wide, pretending I could talk to the sky.
Maybe it was the way I felt energy, palpable, real, between my palms in certain places.
Or how I could feel the mood of a room before anyone spoke, or how horses always told me the truth.

I didn't have language for it then, just instinct, symbols, knowing. Even when the world mocked it, even when boys rolled their eyes, even when friends were uncomfortable with my intensity, I kept the knowing safe, hidden behind poetry and laughter.

I was drawn to the old ways...nature, feathers, crystals, animal signs, candles burned to honour the unnamed. I walked barefoot on dirt roads with friends who felt too much, who fire-twirled under stars, and called each other sisters and brothers.

We were wild and gentle. Half-awake. Half-forgetting. Half-remembering...and the land, it held us. I felt it, even then. That deep pulse in the soil. That alive-ness when you're close to trees and stars and firelight.

There's something sacred about being eighteen and not fitting in. I didn't want what the world told me to want. I wanted truth, freedom, and connection that lived outside the edges of language. I wanted presence over perfection.

"Only in the quiet times, when you sit back and see from hindsight, do you realise you were right all along."

I read that somewhere, or maybe I wrote it. Either way, it stuck.

Because here's the thing babe: You will be told that you're too much. Too emotional. Too intense. Too sensitive. Too different, and you might even believe them for a while.

But one day, you'll realise: You were never too much. You were just remembering who you were before the world told you otherwise.

Your body is ancient. Your bloodline is deep. And your magic? It's not a performance. It's your birthright.

If you're drawn to rituals you don't understand, to songs that feel like déjà vu, to women whose eyes say I see you before they even say hello, follow that thread. You're not imagining it. You're remembering.

I had no mentors. Just friends, moonlight, heartbreak, and a journal full of half-spells. But even that was enough to begin.

So if the wind stirs you, if barefoot earth wakes you, if a horse looks into your soul and doesn't blink, trust it. And if you're unsure of who you are, look to the land. She will remind you. She reminded me, and I haven't forgotten.

With all the quiet power I was only beginning to claim, Your mother *xx*

Letter Four: The Sisterhood That Held Me

To the daughter who will need her people

Dear daughter,

There are people who change you. Not because they teach you anything on purpose, but because they love you in the exact moment you forget how to love yourself.

We were a constellation of tangled hearts and open hands, scattered across couches, mountains, beaches, and backroads. Fruit-picking, barefoot, swapping songs and secrets. Back then, it felt like freedom.
It also felt like survival.

We didn't always say what needed saying, but we danced through the ache together. When the world got loud, we fire-twirled under stars and gave each other wild, sacred names.

One wrote to me:

"My womyn of thunder. You are the storm that washes her, That bathes her in renewed vitality. Mother Nature thanks your spirit."

I didn't know how to receive it then, but I kept it, because some part of me knew I'd need to remember it later.

Back then, we all carried invisible grief. Sometimes we didn't talk about it in depth, just let it leak out sideways, through long drives, tired laughter, rolled smokes and soft glances.

A bit messy. A bit wild. But so real.

We didn't know it at the time, but we were building something sacred: a mirror. A cauldron. A circle. A home.

And yes, sometimes it hurt. Sometimes we broke each other's hearts with silence, or jealousy, or the sharp edge of growing too fast. But we always found our way back. Even when it took years.

Because once someone sees you cry under the stars, or lose yourself in music, or write spells on coasters in pubs, you're tied in a way that doesn't unravel.

If you find people like this, babe, hold them close. Let them witness you. Let them name you. Let them remind you of your own fire when you forget it's there.

And know that not every friendship will last forever, but that doesn't mean it wasn't sacred. Some people walk beside you for only a season, but still leave their laughter in your bones.

"Wild hearts can't be broken"

I wrote that once. We believed it. Mostly. And even when our hearts did break, we knew how to stitch each other back together with music and mischief and moonlight.

So this letter is for the ones who saw me before I saw myself. And for you, so that you never forget you are not meant to do this alone.

With all the tenderness I learned in my friends' arms,
Your mother *xx*

Letter Five: The One Who Romanced Her Own Ruin

To the daughter who confuses fire for love

Dear daughter,

Some parts of me didn't want saving. They wanted to fall, feel, burn all the way down...just to see what survived the ash.

There was a boy. Not the only one, but maybe the one who carved the deepest wound. He didn't mean to, and I didn't mean to give him the blade.

But I handed it over anyway, wrapped in hope, ribboned in self-doubt, offered up like maybe if he held my softness long enough, it would become strength.

It didn't.

"Me and you, we are the turmoil at the base of a wave after it has broke. A storm out at sea."

That's how I described us. Romantic, isn't it? Even my own suffering got the poetic treatment.

"I have to hate you so I can free myself from you."

I wrote that, too. And meant it. But only halfway. Because the truth is, I didn't want to be free. I wanted to be devoured. I wanted to be the girl someone couldn't stop thinking about. The muse. The mystery. The one he could never quite catch. I thought if someone chased me hard enough, maybe I'd finally feel worthy of being caught.

That's the thing about pain, babe. When you carry it long enough, it becomes familiar. So when someone brings you more, it doesn't always feel like harm, it feels like home. And if you're not careful, you can live that cycle for decades before you even realise you're still bleeding from the same wound…trust me, I know.

I clung to him like salt to skin. Even when he ghosted. Even when he lied. Even when my gut screamed and I smiled through it. Because I thought I could alchemise his distance into devotion. Like if I just stayed soft enough, he'd choose me. Like if I broke myself open far enough, he'd finally crawl in.

But that's not how love works. Love doesn't ask you to shrink. It doesn't feed on your confusion. It doesn't hide in half-truths or ignore your silence. It doesn't make you wonder if you're the problem when your soul is starving.

If you ever find yourself aching for someone who only comes close enough to keep you hoping, listen to me:

That's not love.
That's emotional starvation disguised as mystery. That's your own wound reflected back to you.

Walk away. And if you can't walk yet, crawl. And if you can't crawl, cry until you remember how.

You are not a question mark. You are not a second choice. You are not a girl waiting to be saved by a man who doesn't even know how to stay.

It took me years to let go. Longer still to forgive myself for calling it love when it was really just longing that learned how to dress up.

But I did let go. Piece by trembling piece. Until I finally realised I was never meant to be someone's almost. I was meant to be my own holy yes.

So if you ever find yourself playing with fire, make sure it's to keep yourself warm, not to burn yourself down.

With every scar I earned and every flame I've since extinguished,
Your mother *xx*

(©)

Ash in my hair,

salt on my skin,

I leave the fire behind

but carry its glow

in the quiet hollow

of my chest.

CHAPTER TWO

The Quiet Fade

Letters for the liminal space

Letter One: The Girl in the Eye of the Storm

To the daughter who feels herself unravel

Dear daughter,

This earth beneath my feet is trembling. It's subtle to anyone watching, but I feel it. A shift. A cracking. A silent, slow undoing I don't yet have words for.

In my early 20s, I look fine. I smile in photos. I show up to work. I'm in a relationship. I'm "building something". But inside, there's a war.

There is so much noise, expectations, pressure. The daily grind. People keep talking about careers, marriages, finances, futures, but no one tells you what to do when your body wants to disappear. When nothing feels solid. When friendships drift. When you look at the person you're with and realise you don't feel safe, but it would be too messy to leave.
So you stay.

He's fine. He loves me, in his way. But I already know, deep down, I'm not here because of love. I'm here because it's easier. Because I'm afraid of upsetting him. Because someone close to him passed recently and I don't want to be the next person to leave.

I don't say these things out loud, but they live inside me. They twist, and I think that's the scariest part. Not the chaos. But the slow, quiet betrayal of myself.

I miss my friends, scattered now, chasing dreams. I'm here, smiling politely, working jobs that feel like cages, wondering if I'm the only one who didn't get the map. I didn't realise we were living magic back then, barefoot, sun-kissed, talking nonsense and everything that mattered. Now I dance alone in moonlight and hope they think of me too.

This is the storm season. Not dramatic or explosive, just slow erosion. I'm disappearing into someone else's life, travelling on his terms, trying to be who he needs, shrinking so he'll stop being disappointed. I can't remember the last time I laughed from my gut, cried without apologising or did something just for the sheer pleasure of it.

And still, a whisper:

"I am the key to my own spiritual destiny"

I don't know what it means yet, but I feel it in flashes. Lightning over ancient mountains. My feet alone in the sand. Power humming in the womb of a storm. It's not gone, just buried.

So if you ever find yourself here, in the quiet collapse, in the between times, in the place where everything feels upside down and too far gone. Please know this...this isn't the end. It's the middle. The self you feel slipping hasn't died. She's making room for the one you're becoming.

You won't be lost forever, but sometimes you must let go of who you were told to be before you remember who you really are.

With all the love I forgot to give myself,
Your mother *xx*

Letter Two: When I Forgot How to Feel

To the daughter who wonders where her joy went

Dear daughter,

There were years I forgot what it felt like to be happy. Not the performative kind of happy, but the kind that rises from the body like sun through soil…or maybe I never knew it properly to begin with?

Those years were quiet in all the wrong ways. I wasn't falling apart or in love. I wasn't falling into magic. I was just floating, like a woman who left the house and forgot to bring herself.

I travelled, worked, paid bills, got married, smiled at parties, planned trips, and beneath it all was a sense of distance. A life behind glass. Something dulled inside me, and no one noticed, least of all me.

I struggled in the nine-to-five world. I never felt like I was enough, like I fit anywhere. I carried this constant sense of being out of place, no self worth, second-guessing myself, doubting every move, feeling like everything and everyone was surface-level or fake...like I was trying to breathe in a space that wasn't made for me. I wanted confidence, wholeness, to be truly seen...but honestly, I hid too well to be witnessed.

It's strange now, looking back, there was actually so much love around me: cards, letters, small gifts, proof that I was held, that I mattered. I couldn't receive it then though. I didn't know how to. The inner voice was so much louder: "You're not doing enough. You're not being enough. You are not enough". When that voice lives in your bones, it filters everything, even love.

My writing changed too, from incantation to fragments, questions with no answers. Yet still, I wrote, proof I wasn't completely gone.

These weren't dramatic years; they were a soft forgetting. Drifting from myself in increments so small I only noticed when it hurt to come home.

Sometimes the danger isn't the fall, it's in the float. The slow bleed of joy. The quiet ache that says nothing is wrong and nothing is right either.

If that ever happens, babe, pause. Don't ask what should I do? Ask what would make me feel alive again? Then take one small step toward that feeling. Take that one step, and then another, and then another. You deserve more than a half-life and you are never as far away as you may think.

With a softness I'd almost forgotten,
Your mother *xx*

Letter Three: Always Loved (But Couldn't See It)

To the daughter who forgets her worth and finds it again

Dear daughter,

There was so much love, I just couldn't see it. I was wrapped in my own fog, tangled in the stories of not-enough, not chosen, not wanted in the right way, so I missed what was right in front of me. The soft eyes, outstretched hands, friends who stayed longer than they had to, who held space I didn't even know I needed held.

And I couldn't feel any of it because I didn't believe I deserved it. This is what happens when the wound is old, you can be surrounded by warmth and still feel cold; adored and still feel alone; offered softness and only know how to meet it with suspicion or silence.

It wasn't their fault, and it wasn't mine either. I was carrying years, actually generations of quiet forgetting. Of being too much, too sensitive, too wild, too tender. Of being loved for how I made people feel, but not always for who I actually was. So when love came I didn't know how to let it in, I deflected, over-gave, and disappeared.

During this time, I reached for connection in places that felt like love and in many ways, they were. But they were also escape routes from a life I didn't yet know how to breathe inside. I had a habit of choosing what looked warm from the outside but never asked whether it was truly safe to rest in. People loved the version of me that was steady, capable, bright, agreeable...and I let them. Sometimes being wanted, even in a shallow way, felt easier than sitting with the places inside me that felt unseen.

What I didn't realise then was that I had already slipped out of my own skin. I'd become a woman performing "fine," while the deeper truth of me waited quietly underneath, patient and untouched. I was still trying to earn a love I already carried.

So if you ever find yourself in a life that photographs beautifully but aches in private, please pause. Let yourself feel the discomfort without shame. Don't judge yourself for forgetting how to receive. Breathe. The love didn't leave, you just forgot how to let it land. It hasn't disappeared, it's simply waiting for you to turn back toward yourself.

When it lands again, when someone says your name softly, or looks at you like you matter, or sends you a card that makes you cry, don't apologise. Let it in. You're already worthy, even if you can't feel it yet.

With a tenderness I now know how to hold,
Your mother *xx*

◎

There's a silence

that hums between worlds.

Not death. Not birth.

Just the soft ache

of remembering

you were never lost.

CHAPTER THREE

The Long Walk Back

Letters for the quiet remembering

Letter One: Who Am I Without the Mask?

To the daughter who questions everything

Dear daughter,

I began asking questions I wasn't brave enough to answer.

"Who am I when I'm not trying to be liked?

Who am I when no one's watching?

Do I even know what I want, or have I been performing for so long I've forgotten how to feel?"

I didn't have a clear breakdown. Nothing big or dramatic. No flashing neon sign that said you've lost yourself. It was more like waking up in a life that looked okay on the outside, but didn't fit anywhere on the inside.

I felt like I was living sideways. Working jobs that felt like they were going nowhere. Keeping friendships that no longer felt true, and trying to love a life that cherished the mask I wore, but never truly saw the woman underneath. One by one, pieces of me slipped away. My joy, my rituals, my writing voice, my laughter.

And when I looked in the mirror, I couldn't even name what had gone missing, only that it had.

I looked outside of myself: self-help, manifesting, Buddhism, quotes, teachers who promised wholeness. And honestly some of it helped, but most were just bandages on a wound I hadn't touched.

I didn't need fixing, you see. I just needed permission. Permission to feel, to rage, to mourn the woman I thought I'd become, to ask: *"What do I believe when no one is telling me? What do I want when I stop asking what's expected?"*

I'd been everything for everyone. A good partner, the "nice girl", low-maintenance, the woman who never took up too much space. But I was tired of being a projection, of adjusting to the temperature of every room, and of wondering whether my real self even existed anymore.

So I wrote again, not pretty lines, true ones. Raw, unfiltered, doubtful, longing, furious. I stopped trying to be wise and started being honest. In those pages a new voice rose, not polished, not perfect, but true. The woman I was becoming had questions, not answers, and she didn't need to be loved by everyone, just herself.

This is where the remembering starts.

So if you ever find yourself in that space, where everything feels flat, where your life doesn't light you up, where you catch yourself thinking, *"I'm living someone else's dream and I don't know how to get out..."*

Please remember this: you're just between stories. The old doesn't fit anymore and the new has not been written yet. But it will come, word by word, truth by truth, breath by breath. When you finally ask, *"Who am I, really?"* don't rush to answer. Just listen and let yourself become.

With all the love I couldn't yet find inside myself,
Your mother *xx*

Letter Two: The Woman in the Mirror Isn't Me (Yet)

To the daughter who no longer recognises her reflection

Dear daughter,

There was a time I looked in the mirror and didn't see myself. Not poetically, just blank. Like the lights were on, but no one was home.

I was there but unanchored, living, not inhabiting. I had the job, partner, house, routines, but felt like a girl who borrowed someone else's life and didn't know how to give it back. Not miserable, just misplaced.

That's the thing they don't tell you. You don't have to be visibly falling apart to be deeply unwell. I functioned. Said "I'm fine." But alone, the silence echoed.

"The person I show this world is different to the person inside," that's what I wrote. I had split: one part performing, one part fading, neither whole.

Quietly, I questioned everything. I walked like a stranger in my body, trying to remember what lit me up: horses, writing, ritual, connection, bare feet on earth. But it was hard to access that from within the life I had built, a life where I felt I had to explain, justify, apologise, for every soft or strange or sacred part of me.

"You can only see in others what you have inside yourself."

I couldn't see myself clearly because I had surrounded myself with people who didn't know how to see me, who loved the idea of me; who didn't understand my depth; a world that kept rewarding me for hiding. So I smiled. Stayed. Adapted. My spirit grew quiet, not gone, just waiting.

Babe, if your reflection ever feels foreign, don't panic. You're in transition. Shedding. No longer the girl you were and not yet the woman you're becoming. This space is sacred. It's the cocoon, the womb of your becoming. No one gets to tell you who you are. Not a partner, friend, culture, parent…yes, not even me. Only you get to decide what your reflection means. And when you're ready, meet your gaze and ask: *"Who do I want to become, and what part of her already lives in me now?"*

With all the love for myself I was calling back in,
Your mother. *xx*

Letter Three: The One Who Called You In

To the daughter who became the doorway home

Dear daughter,

Before you, I had almost forgotten how to feel, not just love, but aliveness. I was breathing, moving, functioning, but far from myself.

Then something shifted, quietly, softly. You came to me in a dream, or maybe it was a knowing in my belly. I felt you soon, not someday. I told myself it was an accident. It wasn't. I knew. We knew. We barely said the words but they hung between us like a thread already pulled.

It wasn't the perfect time. There was uncertainty, change, a quiet ache I couldn't explain. Still, you chose to come through us, through me, and in doing so, you brought me back.

A friend, a brother wrote me once:
"You are bringing a leader into this world. Realise it. Believe it.

Honour it…If you don't start living like a witch, like the goddess you are, life is always going to be shit for you. You have all the tools. It's all in there. So what are you doing?"…

Those words landed like spells, and I knew some part of me had been waiting for this. For you. For the remembering.

I was three months pregnant when I wrote:
"I can feel myself crossing into mother.

Maidenhood shaped me, through tests, discoveries, travel, friendships, lovers, mistakes, laughter, grief, and all the ways I learned myself.

I'm not leaving her behind.

I'm carrying everything she taught me into this next chapter."

Reading it now I see the line in the sand, the initiation. Your arrival gave me clarity for the first time in years. You cracked something open and I began to remember. I sat in nature again. I wrote. I called old friends, the ones who really knew me. I stopped apologising for softness. I stopped bending myself into someone else's version of a "good woman." I stopped trying to outrun the part of me that felt too much. I made room for you, not only in my body, but in my life and in my truth.

I didn't become a mother the day you were born. I became a mother the moment I said yes to your spirit, even if I couldn't say it aloud, even if I was scared, even if everything around me still felt unsure. You didn't save me;

you reminded me I was worth saving. You were my tether, my mirror, my turning point.

With all the softness I was finally ready to hold,
Your mother *xx*

◎

My bones are full of sky.

What fell away was never wasted.

Everything returns

soil to root,

root to breath,

breath to becoming.

CHAPTER FOUR

The Blood, the Bones, and the Becoming

Letters for the crossing

Letter One: The Portal Is Me

To the daughter who walked me back to myself

"I had a dream:
I was on a journey, gathering something, bones I think. A dingo appeared. I threw bones to him as he followed me through the night. I stopped on a dark roadside, searching. There was something I needed to find. The dingo…and something else. I knew I had to be alone. I ran through dark streets with a knapsack full of clinking bones.

Then came a knowing…he would find me. When we met, he was pure blackness with eyes of blood-red light.
I dropped the bag, and woke."

Dear daughter,

Pregnancy was like taking a breath after years of holding one in. I didn't work. I wandered. I listened. I felt deeply. You slowed me, physically and spiritually. I wrote again… sitting in forests and laying out on mossy rocks. Remembering who I was before I gave so much of myself away. You were growing inside me, and somehow, so was I.

But it wasn't all soft edges and candlelight. It was deep, and raw, and animal. High highs and low lows. Everything in my life sharpened, the beauty, the fear, the truths I'd been avoiding. Parts of my world didn't fit the way they once had.

Parts of me didn't either, and as I opened to you, I felt old identities slipping away. I wrote it one day without meaning to: "*I feel like I'm starting to lose myself.*"

But then, two months before you arrived, I wrote:
"*The forest is alive tonight. Warm air, everything moving. I wonder if you can feel the world through me. I stop. I breathe. And the truth lands: when I fight for the way I think things should be, everything tightens. When I let go, there's space again. I remember I can create. I always could.*"

Even in fear, I was becoming. Not the kind of mother they talk about in books. Not the tidy, glowing one with everything together. But the real kind. The messy, mystical, breaking-open kind. The kind who doesn't know what's next, but says yes anyway.

This is when I understood, the portal wasn't the birth.
It was me.

You walked me back to myself. Through blood and breath. Through fear and awe. Through everything I thought I had lost. And when I dropped the bag of bones, when I let go of who I thought I needed to be, I realised something ancient was still holding me.

You didn't just arrive into my world. You became the world I was rebirthing myself into.

With a love carved into the soil of my being,
Your mother *xx*

Letter Two: The Woman Rewoven

To the daughter who will lose herself and find something even deeper

Dear daughter,

When you were born, the world shifted, not because time stopped or angels sang, though it felt like that, but because I was no longer who I'd been, and I didn't yet know who I'd become.

There's something no one tells you about early motherhood. Not really. They talk about sleep, nappies, milestones, feeding schedules. But they don't talk about the fracture. They don't talk about how birth opens a portal, and that once you've walked through it, you can't return the same.

I loved you with a kind of devotion that startled me. It didn't feel soft and pastel and tidy like the images in magazines. It felt wild. Animal. Like my body had become part forest, part temple, part battlefield. Like I could hold the entire world in my arms, and also collapse under the weight of it.

You were only four months old when my father died. I was just breathing into motherhood, recognising rhythms, your scent in the dark…then grief arrived. One hand held new life; the other was letting go of the one who taught me to walk through the wild.

There were days I'd watch you sleep and wonder how it was possible to feel so full and so hollow at the same time. There were nights I'd cry while folding your tiny clothes, the sound of your breath rising and falling beside me, anchoring me to this moment, even as I ached for the one that was gone.

No one talks about how grief and birth echo each other. The tearing, the threshold, the stretched silence that follows, the way time warps and stretches and never fits quite the same again.

I loved my dad. He was imperfect, complicated, but he was mine. Losing him while becoming your mother shattered something I didn't know was holding me up. And still, you were here, proof. A warm, wriggling reminder that life doesn't pause for our heartbreak. It insists we keep going.

That first year I felt like a ghost in my own skin. People said, "Isn't motherhood amazing?" I nodded. I was lucky, but I was also grieving, becoming, bleeding invisibly. Both can be true.

You were joy and medicine, and I was still broken open. I didn't become whole in a single moment. I stitched myself together one breath at a time, in forest, and silence, and pages of my journal; in small, quiet yeses to feel it all without rushing.

So if you ever find yourself here, holding new life while saying goodbye to something old, whether it's a person, a dream, a version of yourself, know this: feeling "too much" isn't weakness, and needing space isn't failure. You're walking the oldest path there is. Life, death, rebirth. It lives in your body now. The woman on the other side will not be the same, she's deeper, wider, and more real than she's ever been.

With all the pieces I gathered in the dark,
Your mother *xx*

Letter Three: The Woman Between Worlds

To the daughter who awakens inside a life that no longer fits

Dear daughter,

There was a year I barely wrote a word, not because there was nothing to say, but because I couldn't find my edges. I had crossed a threshold. From maiden to mother.

From becoming to being. From dancing barefoot under stars, to walking halls with swollen breasts and tired eyes.

I was quiet, not the peaceful kind; the kind where a soul rearranges itself.

I turned thirty. My body spoke a new language, softened, marked, changed. I grieved the girl-body I once wore like armour, her freedom, hunger, wild edges, recklessness. I missed them all, and so I shed. I shed my dreadlocks, my piercings, versions of myself I had once claimed as gospel. Not because they were wrong, but because they no longer belonged.

Again, my writing shifted from poetry to questions: *"Who am I now? What do I need? What is mine, and what have I inherited?"* I felt the weight of lineage and of expectations, the quiet roles passed down through women who carried more than they should have, or were ever meant to.

I wanted to mother you differently, to give you all the things that I never had. Sometimes I didn't know how. I learned as I went, trying not to lose myself in the process of raising you.

I ached for something I couldn't name, not love or purpose but something older. A rhythm, a circle, a place to be held, not only needed. A sisterhood. A village. A place where women told the truth and motherhood didn't mean invisibility.

My girl, there will be seasons when your soul quietly rearranges itself, and nothing around you feels quite the same. Don't fear that shift. Change is not a failure, it's a kind of truth-telling. We shed who we were so we can grow into who we're meant to be. And in those in-between spaces, you will need women, real women, the kind who sit with you in the mess and remind you of your strength.

But more than anything, you will need yourself. A soft place to land inside your own skin. A way of holding yourself that doesn't depend on anyone rising to meet you or failing you. If you can learn to be that for yourself, everything else becomes steadier.

You're allowed to unravel. You're allowed to begin again. You're allowed to return to yourself, over and over. You're allowed more than just survival. You're allowed to become whole.

With all the gentleness I didn't yet know how to give myself,
Your mother *xx*

Letter Four: The Closing Reflection

To the daughter who will keep walking

Dear daughter,

I wrote these letters as a map, but you'll make your own paths through the wild.

I can only offer what I've learned…that love deepens when it stops performing, that grief is a teacher, and that the most sacred work you'll ever do is remembering yourself.

There is no final arrival. We keep circling back to truth, to softness, to wonder.

Some seasons will strip you bare. Others will bloom in ways you didn't know you could.

Wherever you stand now, whether in longing or in light, know that you come from women who kept going. You are their continuation, their becoming *and* their remembering.

Thank you for finding me here, on these pages. Thank you for reminding me that the story keeps unfolding.

With a love that keeps changing shape,
Your mother, at 46

I love you xx

＠

I have walked myself home

a thousand times.

Each time,

the land remembers first.

Then the horses.

Then me.

www.ingramcontent.com/pod-product-compliance
Lightning Source LLC
Chambersburg PA
CBHW032135080426
42733CB00008B/1079